SPY
CODES
and
Ciphers
BY
SUSAN K. MITCHELL
THE SECRET WORLD OF SPIES
Enslow Publishers, Inc.
40 Industrial Road
Box 398
Berkeley Heights, NJ 07922
USA
http://www.enslow.com

For my wonderful parents, Robbie & Dub

Library of Congress Cataloging-in-Publication Data

Mitchell, Susan K.
Spy codes and ciphers / Susan K. Mitchell.
p. cm. — (The secret world of spies)
Includes bibliographical references and index.
Summary: "Discusses different methods of secret communications used by spies, such as Morse code, the Enigma machine, the Navajo language, and digital steganography, and includes career information"—Provided by publisher.
ISBN 978-0-7660-3709-0
1. Cryptography—Juvenile literature. 2. Ciphers—Juvenile literature. 3. Espionage—Juvenile literature. 4. Spies—Juvenile literature. I. Title.
Z103.3.M58 2011
652'.8–dc22
2010006176

Paperback ISBN 978-1-59845-353-9

Printed in China

052011 Leo Paper Group, Heshan City, Guangdong, China

10 9 8 7 6 5 4 3 2 1

To Our Readers: We have done our best to make sure all Internet Addresses in this book were active and appropriate when we went to press. However, the author and the publisher have no control over and assume no liability for the material available on those Internet sites or on other Web sites they may link to. Any comments or suggestions can be sent by e-mail to comments@enslow.com or to the address on the back cover.

Illustration Credits: Andy Crawford / © Dorling Kindersley, p. 10; Associated Press, pp. 32, 34; Clipart.com, p. 13; Enslow Publishers, Inc., p. 19; Courtesy of Helge Fykse, Norway / National Museum of the U.S. Air Force, p. 23; © iStockphoto.com / Elena Korenbaum, p. 18 (bottom); Library of Congress, pp. 9, 27; Mehau Kulyk / Photo Researchers, Inc., p. 3; National Security Agency, pp. 7, 18 (top), 22; © Pictorial Press Ltd / Alamy, p. 26; Shutterstock.com, pp. 3, 4, 14, 15, 38, 39, 40, 42, 44; © Stephen Rees / iStockphoto, p. 17; © Universal / Everett Collection, p. 29.

Cover Illustration: Mehau Kulyk / Photo Researchers, Inc. (background); Shutterstock.com (lower right image, foreground).

CONTENTS

Chapter 1

Drawing Conclusions

Flashes of light in the darkness. Random puffs of smoke. A series of taps on metal or a jumble of mysterious symbols. To the ordinary person, none of these would mean a thing. They might go completely unnoticed. But to a spy, these could be a very important message—a secret message about the enemy!

As long as there have been governments, militaries, and spies there has been a need to pass along secret coded messages.

Codes are like a language only a few people know. Letters and symbols can be used to mean different things.

Almost anything can be used as a code. Since ancient times, humans have been thinking of new ways to send secret messages. They have been

Wrap Around Codes

One of the oldest codes dates back to ancient Greek times. It uses a tool called a scytale (SKIT-talee). This was a simple, round stick. With it was a long strip of paper. Letters were written down the length of the paper. It looked like nonsense.

Alone, neither the stick nor the paper meant much. However, once the strip of paper was wrapped around the round stick, a message appeared. Both the piece of paper and the size of the stick had to be very carefully measured for the code to work.

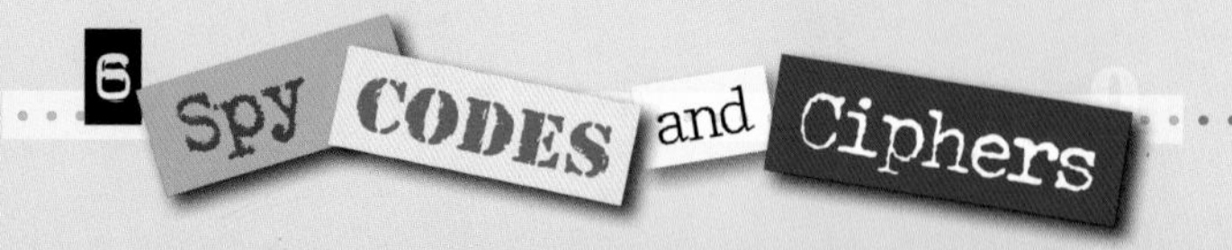

SECRET PROJECT

You can make your own scytale. Take an empty paper towel roll. Wrap a half-inch strip of paper around it. Now write your message across the paper. When you unroll it, the letters will be all jumbled. Have your friends use their own empty paper towel rolls to decode your message!

This is a cipher wheel from the eighteenth century. It is believed that Thomas Jefferson invented this device. Scrambled letters are written on twenty-six wooden wheels mounted on an iron rod. To encode a message, you would spin the wheels to get a message twenty-six letters long, one letter per wheel in a row. Then, you would look at a different line of letters to write down and send to another person. To decode the message, the person would spin his or her cipher wheel to find the same arrangement of letters. Then, he or she would look at the other rows to find a readable message.

hidden in thousands of unusual places. All that really matters is that both the sender and the person receiving the code know the key to decode the message.

Under Their Wings

Lord Robert Baden-Powell had a talent for art. He was a harmless butterfly collector. Or was he? In reality, Lord Baden-Powell was a military spy! His most powerful weapon was his sketchbook.

Lord Baden-Powell worked as an intelligence officer in the British army in the late 1800s. On spy missions, he often disguised himself as a butterfly collector. Then he scouted out the areas near enemy forts. Armed with art supplies and a large net, no one paid him much attention. If he was questioned, Lord Baden-Powell simply asked about different butterflies in the area. The disguise always worked like a charm.

If anyone had looked closely at his drawings, however, they would have seen something far more than a butterfly or moth. Underneath the details of each drawing was a secret code. Plans for the layouts of military forts were hidden in each coded drawing.

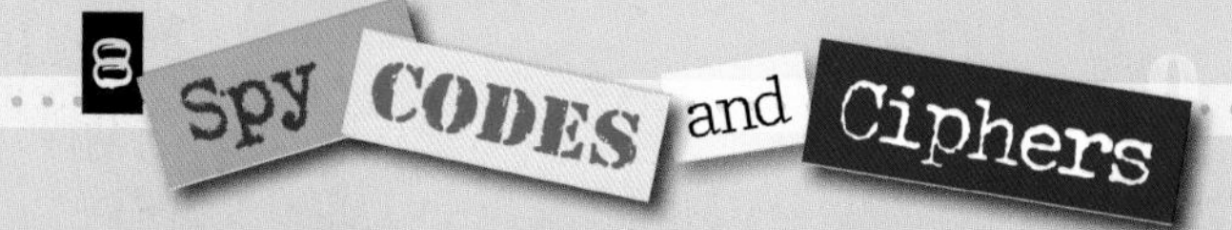

Lord Baden-Powell began the Boy Scouts in Great Britain in 1907.

This is a photograph of Lord Baden-Powell. He used sketches of butterflies, moths, and leaves to send important information to British intelligence about enemy forts.

The layout of a fortress is hidden in this butterfly sketch. The jagged shape around the butterfly's body shows the outline of a fortress. On the wings, marks on the lines show the locations of the guns.

Spots on a butterfly's wing were really locations of large weapons. A moth was really a complete map of a fortress and the area surrounding it.

Nature's Secrets

Lord Baden-Powell did not only use butterfly and moth drawings to hide his secret messages. The central vein on a leaf became the ground around a fortress. Small dots on the leaf showed where machine guns were positioned. Even something like a sketch of a stained glass window could hold secrets.

These sketches gave the British military detailed knowledge about the enemy during the Second Boer War in South Africa. Lord Baden-Powell was so good at acting and spying that he was never caught. His coded drawings were never captured.

The coded sketches gave British troops information that was critical in defeating enemy fortresses. Because of the drawings, they knew how to take out the enemy's weapons. They knew the best place to attack. They knew the weaknesses of the fort—all because of a seemingly harmless drawing!

Unsolved Mysteries

Some codes are so complex they remain unsolved even today! Not all of them are ancient. In 1990, artist Jim Sanborn created a huge sculpture for the Central Intelligence Agency (CIA). It sits outside the headquarters in Langley, Virginia. The sculpture is called *Kryptos*. On it are four coded messages. They are a seemingly random jumble of letters.

Code breakers have tried for years to figure out all four codes. The first three codes took years to crack. As of 2010, no one has solved the fourth section of the code on *Kryptos*.

Chapter 2

Connecting the Dots

Not all codes are written down. Imagine hiding a message in a series of clicks or flashing lights! That is exactly how Morse code works. Inventor Samuel F. Morse created the code in the early 1800s. Morse invented a machine called a telegraph. He found he could tap out a message using electricity. The electric impulses traveled by wire to another waiting telegraph machine.

A short tap is called a dot. A longer tap is called a dash. These dots and dashes are combined to

Samuel F. Morse invented Morse code. It is a very easy system to learn.

represent each letter of the alphabet. They also can represent numbers and punctuation. The system is very easy to learn. It is also amazingly fast! A trained person can send or decode twenty to thirty words each minute.

In 1844, Morse unveiled his invention in the United States Congress. The government instantly saw how important this could be. The telegraph machine itself was very inexpensive. The Morse code system was quick and efficient. It was not long before other countries developed their own versions of Morse code as well.

Following the Dress Code

However, Morse code was only designed to improve communication across long distances. It was quick. It was easy. It was not, however, very secret. It had worked well during the Civil War. However, by the time World War II raged, newer and more secret codes had to be developed.

Morse code did still have some advantages. While Morse code is normally sent electrically or by light, it can be written down also. The dots and dashes can be written down to create a message.

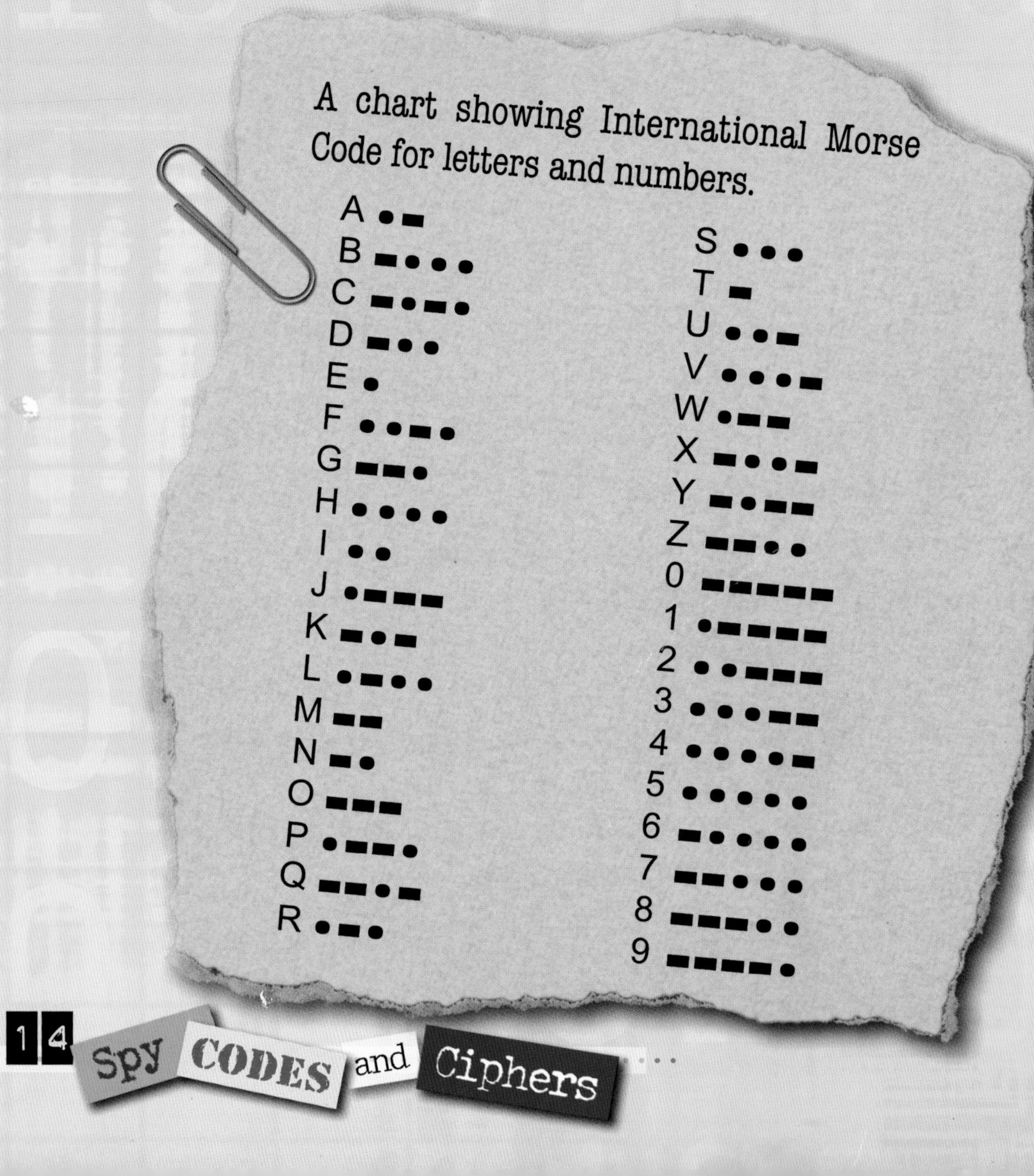

A chart showing International Morse Code for letters and numbers.

This person taps Morse code on an old telegraph machine.

Once written down, the code could be easily hidden in everyday items. The German Nazis did just that. Their spies used written Morse code to pass along secret messages. They hid the coded messages in fashion designs.

They sent what seemed like normal sketches of models wearing the latest fashions. At first glance, the drawings seemed harmless. However, these were no ordinary models. Patterns of dots and dashes were sketched into the clothing. What appeared to be polka dots on dresses were really coded messages.

Messages were cleverly written onto sketches of hats, gowns, and other outfits. This did not fool

SECRET FACT

The most well known Morse code message is • • • – – – • • •. This stands for S.O.S. It is a commonly used call for help even today. Despite common beliefs, the code does not mean Save Our Ship or Save Our Souls.

Allied troops for long. The British secret service figured out the plot. They were quickly able to send agents to intercept the Nazi messages.

Breaking codes has always been important for the military. Today, however, it is also important for many businesses. As computers and computer programs get more advanced, so does the need for people who can create or break codes.

S.O.S. - Morse code today

Morse code has been used longer than any other code system. It has been used in some form for more than 150 years. As technology and codes advanced, Morse code became less frequently used. Today, it is mainly used by amateur radio operators and by pilots.

The letters SOS do not actually stand for anything. Knowing Morse code, SOS was an easy way to remember that three dots, three dashes, and three dots was a call for help.

Tales from the Cryptanalyst

As long as there have been codes, there have been code breakers. A person who breaks codes is called a cryptanalyst. They are usually very good at math. It is their job to analyze a code and figure it out.

One of the most famous cryptanalysts was William F. Friedman. He worked for the U.S. Army. He led the Signals Intelligence Service (SIS) during the 1930s. This was the army's code breaking unit. The unit was so secret that many did not know it even existed!

Fair and Square

One of the earliest and simplest codes is from Greek times. It is the Polybius square. It is also called the Polybius checkerboard. This code uses numbers to represent letters. This type of code is called a substitution cipher. It can be changed to fit different needs and alphabets. It can also be made as easy or as difficult as needed.

A square grid is assigned numbers vertically and horizontally. A simple 5x5 grid will work for the English alphabet. Letters are then placed on the grid. The word C-A-T becomes 13-11-44.

This can also be used as a "knock code." During the Vietnam War, prisoners would use the Polybius square numbers to knock out messages to each other on the walls of their huts.

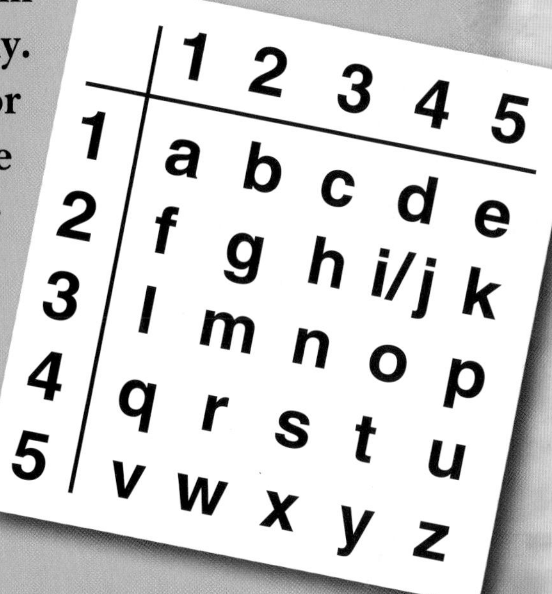

	1	2	3	4	5
1	a	b	c	d	e
2	f	g	h	i/j	k
3	l	m	n	o	p
4	q	r	s	t	u
5	v	w	x	y	z

An example of a Polybius square.

SECRET FACT

The U.S. Navy still uses signal lamps to transmit Morse code during times of radio silence.

While not widely used for spying, Morse code can still be very useful. It is one of the most versatile code systems in the world. Morse code has come in handy in many emergency situations. It can be very helpful when there is no other way to communicate.

During the Vietnam War, Jeremiah Denton was captured by North Vietnam troops. He was videotaped and forced to say he was being treated well. Major Denton said the words he was supposed to say even though it was a lie. His eyes, however, told a different story. He used Morse code to send a secret message to our military. While he spoke, he used eye blinks to spell T-O-R-T-U-R-E.

Chapter 3

Cracking the Enigma

It looked like a clunky typewriter. It was full of lights, wheels, and wires. But the Enigma machine was so much more. This strange machine helped the Nazis create almost unbreakable codes during much of World War II.

The Enigma machine used a system of electrical connections and lights. Wheels and rotors spun as a keyboard operator typed in a coded message. What made the codes so hard to crack is that they were constantly changing!

During World War II, the Nazis used Enigma machines to encode secret messages.

There were many different combinations that could be used to make codes. The only way to break the code was to have another Enigma machine and a code book. So even if the Nazis' enemies captured a machine, it would be useless without a book. This gave the Nazis an advantage during the war. It was an advantage that was not to last, however.

Luftwaffe (German Air Force) troops use two Enigma machines, perhaps to encode and decode messages at the same time.

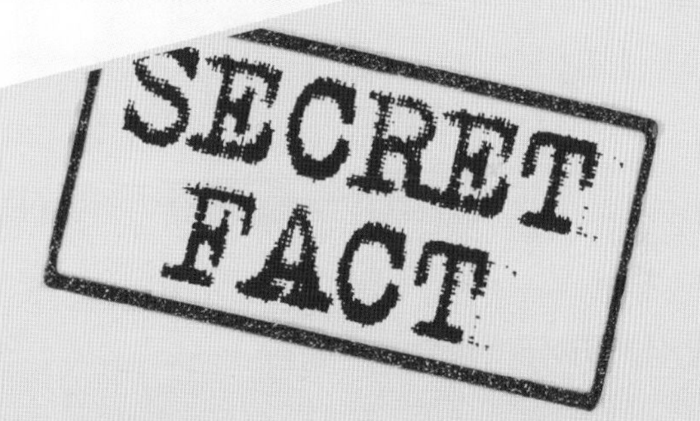

The first Enigma machine was built in 1918. At the time, the German military was not interested in it. The military did not start building them until 1926.

Enigmatic Double-Cross

Whenever there is a code, there are others who are trying to break it. The Enigma machines were no different. One of the biggest breaks for the Allied forces was spy Hans Schmidt. He worked for the German government. Schmidt decided to steal Enigma codes and secrets. He then sold them to France.

Unfortunately, this information by itself was not enough to help French and British forces. They asked for help from the Polish government and military. The Polish forces quickly realized the only way to break the code was to try and build a machine that worked like an Enigma. It was close but not exact.

They hired cryptologist Marian Rejewski. He was able to figure out the basics of how the Enigma worked. Unfortunately, without the daily changing setting, he was only able to figure out part of the puzzle.

Dropping the "Bomb"

All of this helped the Allied forces get closer to defeating the Nazis. The final step was to create an actual Enigma machine. These replicas were nicknamed "bombes" because of the ticking sound they made. Each one that was made was better than the one before it. These machines got the Allied forces closer to breaking the Nazi Enigma codes.

The best and closest Enigma replica was built by the British code breaker, Alan Turing. This version was based on all the previous copies. This work of the Allied forces had seriously weakened the Enigma's code power.

Codes Submerged

All of this work helped crack many of the Enigma's codes. However, it often took several days just to decode a few messages. They needed a way to discover the Nazi secrets sooner. This was especially true when it came to the German submarines called U-boats.

Almost every German U-boat had an Enigma machine. The Nazis knew they risked being captured so they had plans in place to prevent such a raid. German sailors were instructed on how to destroy the Enigma machines. They were told to throw the machines overboard if they were attacked. As a last resort, they were even ordered to sink their U-boat and avoid being captured.

The Brains at Bletchley Park

Behind the walls of a large British brick mansion, spies and scientists were at work. It was called Bletchley Park. During World War II, this was the main base for government code breakers. It was also home to one of the earliest known computers.

In 1943, Tommy Flowers designed the Colossus. It was one of the earliest versions of a computer. It was designed to read encrypted German messages during the war. The Colossus was a huge machine! In 1994, a team recreated the giant machine for Bletchley Park, which is now a museum.

COLOSSUS

The Colossus machine was used to read Nazi codes at Bletchley Park during World War II.

A German U-boat beached on the south coast of England, photographed between 1914 and 1918, during World War I.

SECRET FACT

In 2000, one of the few surviving Enigma machines was stolen from Bletchley Park. The thief asked for £25,000 ransom. At the time, that was more than $35,000. Police used codes hidden in newspapers to catch the thief.

Even with the best plans in place, many of the U-boats were captured by Allied forces. Enigma machines and code setting lists were seized. This helped the Allies decode Enigma messages quicker than ever before. This work helped end World War II many years earlier than anyone thought possible.

Enigma Movie Magic

Recovering Enigma machines has been a popular subject in movies. The German film *Das Boot* and the U.S. film *U-571* have both portrayed the invasion of German U-boats to capture Enigma machines. Not all of the films have been considered accurate. Even the code breakers at Bletchley Park have been film subjects in the 2001 film *Enigma*.

Matthew McConaughey, Erik Palladino, and Jack Noseworthy portray American soldiers who board a German U-boat to capture its Enigma machine in the 2000 film *U-571*.

Chapter 4

Lost Languages

The strongest code is one that no enemy can figure out. What code could be better than a language almost no one knows? That was exactly what Philip Johnston thought during World War II. Johnston was not a Navajo. He had, however, grown up on a Navajo reservation. He also spoke their language.

Johnston heard that the army had used American Indian soldiers to pass codes in World War I.

He met with the Marine commanders to share his idea. At the time of World War II, few people understood the Navajo language. Johnston knew this could be the code that the U.S. Marines needed.

In Their Native Tongue

In early tests, the Navajo code was a success. It proved to be much quicker than codes produced by machines. The first code talkers joined the Marines in 1942. The Navajo language was an unwritten language. It had no alphabet or symbols. It was very difficult to understand.

SECRET FACT

Adolf Hitler sent anthropologists to secretly study the American Indians before World War II. It turned out to be a nearly impossible job. This was because there were so many different languages and dialects.

The code used Navajo words in place of letters of the English alphabet. The letter "A," for example might be *wol-la-chee*, which means ant. Many letters of the alphabet had at least two or three Navajo words that corresponded with them. *Bel-la-sana*, which meant apple, could also stand for the letter "A." This helped make sure the code could not easily be broken.

The Navajo code talkers also used their own native words as substitutions for English words. In some cases, there were no words in the Navajo language for some of the American military terms. They had no

Navajo code talkers serving with the U.S. Marine Corps use a portable radio in the jungles of New Guinea (now Papua New Guinea) in December 1943.

word for "tank" or "fighter plane." The code talkers had to come up with substitution words. For example, tanks were called *chay-da-gahi*, which meant tortoise.

The Few and the Proud

By 1945, more than four hundred Navajo soldiers were serving in the U.S. Marine Corps as code talkers. They were stationed throughout the Pacific area where the U.S. was fighting with the Japanese forces.

Guilt by Association

The Japanese forces successfully captured one Navajo. He was a soldier in the U.S. Army, however. He was not a marine code talker. He was tortured by the Japanese. They forced him to try and translate the Navajo messages.

The soldier had not gone through the code talker training. He had absolutely no idea what the coded messages meant even though he spoke the Navajo language!

The Japanese were extremely good at breaking most codes. One of the codes they could not break, however, was the Navajo codes. It was very frustrating for the Japanese. During the battle of Iwo Jima, the code talkers worked for days. They sent code around the clock. They sent and received more than eight hundred messages with zero errors. Their work helped win the battle.

Navajo code talkers aboard the USS *Intrepid* on November 10, 2009. During World War II, they helped the United States win two battles on Iwo Jima and other battles in the Pacific.

Tribal Nation

The Navajo language was not the only American Indian language to be used as code by the military. The first recorded use of American Indians as code talkers was during World War I. Cherokee and Choctaw soldiers helped send messages between the troops. Comanche soldiers worked as code talkers during the invasion of Normandy in World War II.

Both German and Japanese troops were completely baffled by their language code. It could not be broken! These soldiers were an extremely important part in winning each war. Unfortunately, they were not recognized for their efforts at the time. It took until the twenty-first century for many of them to receive honors from the United States.

Some spoken codes just seem like silliness. During World War II, coded messages were sent during radio broadcasts. A nonsense phrase like "The eagle wears striped pajamas," for example, would only mean something to the person who knew the code words.

Chapter 5

Good Will Hacking

Times have changed for codes and code breakers. Gone are the days of scrambled letters wrapped around sticks. Codes are rarely hidden in drawings of butterflies or fashion models. Today's codes have gone high-tech.

Much of the code breaking today is done by computer. The Internet has forever changed the way information is sent and received. Spies are not the only ones to realize this.

Terrorists use this technology to send and break codes as well. Criminals use it, too.

Many modern-day spies have to be computer experts. Messages can be hidden almost anywhere on the Internet. They just need to be encrypted. This means that they are changed to look like ordinary computer files. This new way of passing along codes is called steganography. Terrorist groups often hide messages in digital pictures or music files.

What may look like a simple computer file may actually be encrypted information that criminals can use to do harm.

"White hat" computer hackers work with the government to fight against computer-savvy terrorists.

Hiring a Hacker

Having a computer hacker working for you might sound crazy. However, the CIA, the Federal Bureau of Investigation (FBI), and many intelligence agencies around the world actually hire them. They are called "white hat" hackers. This means they use their computer hacking knowledge to help law enforcement instead of to commit crimes.

These agencies know that the terrorists have their own computer hacker experts. In order to fight back, they have to make sure they have good people who can use the same skills to prevent attacks.

You've Got Mail

Even e-mail or a simple photo can be used as a coded message. As long as the criminals have an encryption program, they can scramble their message. Unfortunately, these types of programs are easy to get. Here is how it works. Pictures on the computer are really created by a series of dots. Inside the dots are a string of letters and numbers. Computers read these letters and numbers and then put them back together. This is what creates the image on the computer screen.

A coded message can be hidden in those letters and numbers using very simple software. When the picture is sent, the person who receives the picture is able to decrypt—or undo—the hidden information and get the message.

A New Age in Spying

Technology has changed many of the ways in which spies work. The World Wide Web has given the bad guys a million places to hide. Many spies pore over pages on the Internet. They listen to hours of cell phone conversations. They watch video after video found on the Web.

Program codes can contain hidden messages.

In fact, some of that work is actually done by other computers instead of people. These computers quickly process and decode huge amounts of information. They all do this in hopes of catching the hidden messages terrorists may be sending, then breaking the code.

More and more, terrorist groups are using social networking sites. They also use chat rooms and blogs to pass along messages. Spies today work undercover on these Internet sites to discover secret messages. As technology grows, the world of spies must be ever changing.

SECRET FACT

In 2009, the FBI caught a terrorist who planned to blow up a Dallas skyscraper. They were able to find out his plans by using a chat room. He was arrested before he could carry out his plans.

Spies Like Who? A Career in Codes

Think you might never use math in real life? You will if you work as a code breaker. Today's cryptanalysts usually have college degrees in math. They also might have degrees in computer science or engineering. Many of them have higher degrees like a PhD.

Some agencies, like the National Security Agency (NSA), have special programs to train code breakers. Governments are not the only places they can work either. Many large businesses hire code experts. Banks and universities are just a few places where they might work. The average salary for a cryptanalyst is around $76,000 per year.

If you are good at math and with computers, and you would like to help people, a career as a cryptanalyst may be a good choice.

Glossary

Allied forces—Countries that fought against the Nazi and Japanese forces during World War II.

cryptologist—A person who studies secret writing like codes and cipher systems.

decode—To solve a code and discover its meaning.

decrypt—To decode.

disguise—To change one's appearance to hide a true identity.

encrypt—To use a secret code, as in computer files, to hide a true meaning.

hacker—A person who is an expert in breaking computer codes.

replica—An exact copy of an object.

steganography—The act or science of writing hidden messages.

symbol—Something used to represent something else.

To Find Out More

Books

Blackwood, Gary. **Mysterious Messages: A History of Codes and Ciphers.** New York: Dutton Children's Books, 2009.

Blake, Spencer. **Spyology: The Complete Book of Spycraft.** Cambridge, Mass.: Candlewick Press, 2008.

Earnest, Peter and Suzanne Harper, in association with the Spy Museum. **The Real Spy's Guide to Becoming a Spy.** New York: Abrams Books for Young Readers, 2009.

Gilbert, Adrian. **Codes and Ciphers.** Laguna Hills, Calif.: QEB Publishing, Inc., 2008.

Langley, Andrew. **Codes and Codebreaking.** Mankato, Minn.: Smart Apple Media, 2010.

Scott, Carey. **Spies and Code Breakers: A Primary Source History.** Pleasantville, N.Y.: Gareth Stevens Pub., 2009.

Internet Addresses

Central Intelligence Agency (CIA): Break the Code

<https://www.cia.gov/kids-page/games/break-the-code/index.html>

National Security Agency (NSA) CryptoKids™: America's Future Codemakers and Codebreakers

<http://www.nsa.gov/kids/home.shtml>

Secret Codes for Kids: Build Your Own Cipher Wheel

<http://www.topspysecrets.com/secret-codes-for-kids.html>

Index